and
most
Best
iting

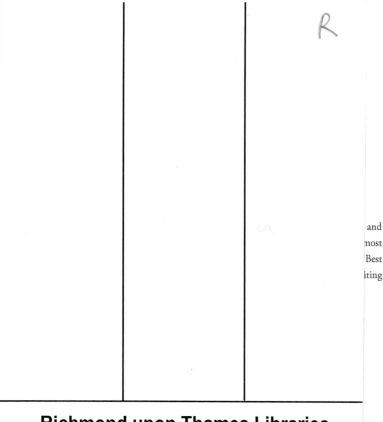

Richmond upon Thames Libraries

Renew online at www.richmond.gov.uk/libraries

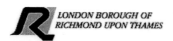
LONDON BOROUGH OF
RICHMOND UPON THAMES

Reckless Paper Birds

John McCullough

Penned in the Margins

LONDON

PUBLISHED BY PENNED IN THE MARGINS
Toynbee Studios, 28 Commercial Street, London E1 6AB
www.pennedinthemargins.co.uk

The right of John McCullough to be identified as the author of this work has been asserted by him in accordance with Section 77 of the Copyright, Designs and Patent Act 1988.

This book is in copyright. Subject to statutory exception and to provisions of relevant collective licensing agreements, no reproduction of any part may take place without the written permission of Penned in the Margins.

First published 2019

Printed in the United Kingdom by TJ International

ISBN
978-1-908058-63-8

This book is sold subject to the condition that it shall not, by way of trade or otherwise, be lent, re-sold, hired out, or otherwise circulated without the publisher's prior consent in any form of binding or cover other than that in which it is published and without a similar condition including this condition being imposed on the subsequent purchaser.

CONTENTS

ACKNOWLEDGEMENTS

I am grateful to the editors of the following magazines and anthologies where poems from this collection have appeared: *Alice* (Poetry Shed, 2016), *B O D Y*, *Disclaimer*, *Divining Divas* (Lethe, 2012), *Litter*, *The Morning Star*, *The Moth*, *Perverse*, *Poetry London*, *Poetry Wales*, *The Rialto*, *Stand*, *The White Review*. 'The Zigzag Path' was commissioned by the BBC for National Poetry Day 2018 and was made into a video poem that appeared on the BBC Arts website.

I wish to thank the members of my writing group in Hove who have looked at drafts of a number of these poems: Maria Jastrzebska, Jackie Wills, Robert Hamberger, Janet Sutherland, Bernadette Cremin and Robert Dickinson. I'm grateful, too, for feedback from Kate Potts, Holly Hopkins, Dai George, Alison Winch, Rowena Knight, David Tait, Karen Goodwin, Deborah Turnbull, Daisy Behagg and Sea Sharp.

NOTES

'Soulcraft' takes its title from both a book by Bill Plotkin and a popular series of action RPG games. 'Michael' was written after figures were released showing Brighton has the second largest population of rough sleepers in England, with a quarter of all young people who are homeless identifying as LGBT.

Reckless
Paper
Birds

The Zigzag Path

The day connives and you think you cannot live here,
in your body, alone and rushing forward all the time

like a silty river. All you wanted was to find a home
beside the souls of white roses and hurt no one

but the light keeps shifting. An invisible broom
keeps flicking you out from cover. You roll up

at each destination with a different face, as wrong
as the beech tree in Preston Park hung with trainers,

a museum of tongues. The day connives, but this dirt
is proof of trying. The chalk path you never longed for

zigzags through cowslips no one asked to throng.
In the park, a robin has built its nest inside a Reebok,

the shoe's throat packed with moss and a crooked
whisper of grass that says *I can, I can, I can.*

Flock of Paper Birds

I needed the God of my childhood to be useful
    so I folded him, shaped his pages into wings.

Cranes at first, then more challenging roosters,
    swallows, owls. I pinched edges, split clauses

to make word plumage. I fractured Leviticus
    with pleats. Now toucans mount doves

on the kitchen counter, near an unholy pile
    of geese, cloacas gaping, beaks jabbing everywhere.

Birds plummet from shelves without bothering
    to flap, remember nothing. Ink blurs,

feathers yellow. They drown in baths, rip luridly,
    turn up mangled in the hallway, footprints

across their necks. Mostly, they're individuals,
    smoothly indifferent to each other's fates,

though now and then some prop up neighbours
  if they topple, and when I lie with a visitor

beneath my quilt, incubating his glorious buttocks,
  the flock discover their throats and sing together

while I guide my tongue along warm creases
  and the tight sheet of his body unfolds.

Tender Vessels

I keep trying to slip away through the crowd
but history won't take its mouth off my body.
What was exacted on someone else's softness,
his cuttable flesh, is always about to happen here.
The vague kinship which exists between tender men
glowing with thirst starts in awareness of this,

how we're unstitched by tongue prints, resurrections.
Standing in a street party one Pride, I saw a figure
stomp through, fists raised, and strike three boys.
They dropped to the ground, clutching their heads.
I witnessed everything, squeezed a stranger's shoulder,
then, fifteen minutes on, my body was distracted

utterly by the smell of oranges. The unspeakable
scrapes a fingernail across my neck but I can only
concentrate so long before I wind up decanting
myself into the nearest fizzing light: Instagram,
house music. It's like those inventors who tried to devise
a spray-on cast for broken bones, created Silly String.

But there are remedies worse than squirting
metres of sticky mayhem across a jubilant face,
outcomes bleaker than attempting, despite the scissors,
to inhabit this twenty-first-century skin.
I live in a dream of plummeting from the earth's
tallest building without ever having felt more beautiful

because I'm not the only one falling. I'm in a crowd,
a loose democracy of descent, velocity with its hands
all over our bodies, but not enough to stop us
gossiping and blowing kisses as we speed
through the air together, reckless paper birds.
They will find us with our beaks wide open.

Stationery

September is going all out to ease us in.
    The clouded sky is a whiteboard for helpful diagrams,
        the first cool air as welcome as your hand inside my jeans.

Autumn zips round with its orange highlighter
    and you provide nifty shocks and marshmallows,
        leaving pornographic Post-its that ask me to rendezvous,

please, for hot chocolate. I am the type of man
    who likes unnecessary displays of manners,
        who appreciates thank you cards, warning signs,

a forest of regretful notices for building works.
    I admire rows of ginkgos that lose all their foliage
        in one drop to form a Yellow Brick Road.

I am a desperate Lion today, stalking Scarecrow.
    I chew biros, glimpse at my watch too often. I was so afraid
        of being late to see you, once, I turned up six days early.

Love is horrific like that. First it's a rabbit, then a duck,
    then it's a ravenous, one-eyed sock puppet;
        but the rest is yoghurt adverts. And you fasten my thoughts

with the most beautiful paperclips, even the filthy ones,
    like the time I saw a grove of ripening chilli plants
        become a rainbow of penis trees. *Do you wish to continue*,

says the voice of a self-service checkout. Yes, yes I do.
    Between the shops, the sea snuggles under its blue leaves.
        The clock tower waits patiently for Christmas,

a familiar figure below it waggling his arms
    to lure me over. Succeeding. Your skilful face punches
        a giant hole in the day and I jump through it.

Nuthatch

Yes, this really is me, lumbering

in joggers and a twenty-year-old body

if I could, swap for something

It gathers sweat in unseasonal heat.

its blood, observed by a man in dark

who lives in the sky like a blizzard

powder and home gyms, who only

the air from the Rolex he keeps on

For ten weeks, I've pictured the least

by two thousand rogue butterflies

through his keyhole in wisps.

past a kidney-shaped swimming pool

a leaky skin suit I'd return to the shop

more cyborg, chrome-plated.

The back of my neck reveals

glasses two decades older

reversed, an upward vortex of white

knows how to soar. Light slashes

in bed. We're not going to make it.

offensive escapes: being carried off

or quietly evaporating so I can steal

Each night, I pause on the threshold.

Then, in the corner of his garden

a nuthatch sprints beak-first down

the grooved bark of a poplar

like a blue roof slate

dropping straight to the soil

a trick of geometry that depends

on sturdy toes, long claws.

And I know it must be this way.

I will learn to fall with my eyes

fixed on the ground, will trust

the honeycomb of bones

I can't see, my feet in touch

with other textures and contours

I will grow into, that will grow

into me as my form descends

leaving the brittle heights behind.

Jay

There are hours when the walls
      of this avenue open. In the flat opposite,
two men in a king-sized bed are woken
      on each other's shores by a third
who sets down a tray of coffee,
      spreads his arms like a prankish flying
squirrel, then glides between them.
      The undergrad above is deconstructing
brands of bubble bath, their genders.
      What can you do if you're Titanium
and Marshmallow? They hold
      a bottle of each next to the ceiling
and Niagara themselves into the water.
      Elsewhere, a Roman empress tucks away
the handcuffs, cheery-byes her milkmaid
      who'd better gazelle it or the vegetarian
shoe shop will never swing wide its doors.
      This is the unforeseen road of my thirties,
where mauve armpit hair and sparklers

are ordinary, where I have landed up
a gardener, a not-always-disgusting
    citizen, where an ice blue flash
of jay's wing swoops through the morning
    as if this were someone else's life.
An ice blue that is really bands
    of graduated blues. A swoop
that is a bird averse to leaving
    a conifer's shelter, banking on gravity
and its body to merge into one arc
    while the image dives through my eye
then vanishes into unmapped streets.

Tumbleweed

'You cannot detain and persecute people who simply do not exist in the republic.'

Spokesman for President Ramzan Kadyrov on Chechnya's concentration camps for gay men

They cluster beside the house at midnight,
a crowd of spiky globes piling against windows,
blocking out the moon. Skeletons of Russian thistle,

their dry fingers score glass, scrape paint
from the sills. It's too much. I cannot stay inside
and listen. I open the front door and greet them

with a chainsaw. I slice the curled spines
then raze the fragments with a propane torch.
There is no other way to handle what does not exist.

It is the dead ones that travel, that disperse
the seed. March gales drive them west,
their bones bouncing over the Channel,

harassing the coast. They accumulate
along ditches and railway tracks. Lately,
I've started noticing them elsewhere:

beneath a park bench, wedged on top
of broken glass, knotted around electric fences.
I fall asleep, counting as they hurry over gates.

I dream I'm flying a jet and encounter them,
huge as airships, blundering into my path.
They bump against the fuselage, wake me

and I drift to the window, their nails scratching
and scratching as if I'm meant to understand.
I look down while my fingers lengthen and twist,

while I bend forward and my spine
completes its arc so my cloud of thorns
can gently tangle, begin to roll.

Queer-Cole

You tumbled into my palm   in a trickle of sterling
bad coin   foul queen   though I didn't notice.

I pocketed you   conveyed you   like your Sedan chair
respectfully slotted you   into vending machines that coughed

you out.   You winked at me   from a change tray
and abruptly   I spotted everything about you

was wrong   your weight   your ill-defined milled edge
your obverse skewed.   Not copper zinc nickel   but lead

sprayed with gold paint.   Too shiny.   *Queer-cole*
they used to say   meaning counterfeit or base money

what ends up improperly   beside your person   tilting
the system   forcing each wall   mutilating the weather.

Fucking queer   a voice in the Watford crowd snarled
as my lips brushed Ryan's cheek.   There I was   my mouth

mimicking legit   my hoodie cap trackies   like a man's
but on close inspection awry   my voice too light

edges blurred.   Flickery.   I carry this awareness in my blood
how simply I'm revealed   as undermining the currency

warping the ceiling.   Now coin   I keep you squirrelled
in my wallet's secret section.   You are my talisman

return me to what I am   no pink pound   but queer-cole
rebel head   wonky origin   dangerous minting.

Flamingo

We prefer shallow water,
gathering in hundreds at night clubs
by the shore. The powder cakes
we bring say EAT ME and we do,
gobbling up beakfuls till our heads turn
upside-down. We don't know
how Sia and Audrey Hepburn joined us,
pirouetting across the floor. And who
invited the clouds? We don't mind.
Our origin is in fire. We are invincible,
even if we're imaginary figures
in some Red King's dream, even if
we may be losing it, may in fact just be me
standing on one perilous leg beside
the speaker, waiting for the rain to stop.

Aether

In one anonymous seventeenth-century painting   a naked man
opposes the five elements.   He stands primed on sodden ground

before a blazing oak   its terriers of flame   nursed by the air.
Above him in the distance   aether   more subtle than light

more indifferent   the space that allows the gods to breathe.
The man must use his five senses   be resourceful   not yield.

A few centuries later   on the train from London to Brighton
I'm wedged in   behind five mates on a stag night.

One does *the gay voice*   making kissing sounds
another yelling *Backs to the walls!*   again and again.

The rest smirk   each fuelled   by translucent permissions.
I stare at my palm   at the curve where yesterday

your lips nestled.   I plunge my face into the woollen scarf
I borrowed   its deep smell of you.   Outside treeless fields

hover silently in half-light   stalks of tall grass dipping
and wheeling   beneath them a scattering   of unseen beasts

voles and pheasants which thrive undercover   which press
their bodies together and hurtle   through numberless hours.

Notes for a Cheery Post-Apocalyptic Short

When I moved to Brighton, my clocks changed their rhythms.
Five penises decide to live together under a little blanket.

Queer men sprang up like careless tulips on every bus.
The names of the penises are Sven, Basil, Rock, Leo and Jorge.

I woke on the beach with strangers, in a tangle of Adidas and dread.
They tremble alone under weeds till Sven gathers them.

It was like relearning the full array of punctuation marks.
The penises have no idea how they came to be detached.

The breakthrough was forest yoga, honeying with nimble bears.
Discovering the blanket leads to questions around penis gods.

I fell in with a filmmaker who had a weakness for adult fairy tales.
Mistaken for a starfish, they glimpse their collective future.

I've not seen him for years but often remember his soft voice.
The blanket remains silent, its own agenda unfinished.

orientate

The beautiful map is wrong. That city you hankered after for years—dreaming its textures, peopling cinemas and delis, knowing everyone's name—ballooned off in the night. The family of strangers who should have enclosed you at the station in a thicket of gleaming limbs misheard and went to meet you in a different epoch, and all you have is a battered suitcase and a website designer called Jeremy who sneers at your love of Pizza Hut and the next morning tells you, *please piss off out of my flat.*

What can you say when you ask the world for space to frolic and acres appear on every side, carry on to the horizon? No walls or barriers, only there are, just not where expected: three bricks in the middle of a library, a shop selling gates, a door lying flat on the beach.

You go round with a wheelbarrow, chucking in what you can, showing up, skinny-jeaned, with your rubble at anyone's party. Three months in, though, when you look down, what you have is mostly a collection of disembodied hands. You're still carting them around, the remnants of a dreamed city, cherished pieces of the humans you imagined you'd meet.

You stop pushing and rest the barrow on its side. The pile of flesh tumbles to the ground, fingers uselessly grasping: thumbs that will never stroke you, palms that can't form a foothold. You sit among them, closed fists, random pointings, shadow puppets that seem to have started a little play.

Flavour

FILL UP WITH A FULL ENGLISH! shouts the greasy spoon
but today it is lovelier to be unEnglished, unafraid to lift chopsticks
from a bowl of pho and snatch passing mechanics or rain clouds,

gulp them down whole. In Brighton, there are many ways
to guzzle the scenery. You can upgrade your body
and slink along the pavements as a giant tongue.

In my first week here, I had a one-night stand
with a choreographer who had a wound fetish,
his painted skin a lavascape of open fractures, latex burns.

I licked his armpits and he charred my hand
with a colour wheel of make-up. It was a bandaged adventure
and if the sky were wallpapered lime and crimson tomorrow

I wouldn't be surprised. A shred of extra zest is always welcome.
My bowl is empty but my days are full as they are
for these plastic cats that keep raising huge paws,

not stopping to ask why they're beckoning, just giving themselves
to the act, their gaping mouths awaiting equally every flavour
luck brings, each scrap of the streets' fire and water.

Nervous Systems

The politicians loiter in a café by the conference centre:
lanyards, collusion and friendless scoops of cherry ripple

spooned onto tongues between fringe events, rebirths.
They skulk like cod behind paper cups and notebooks,

every other word underlined. Danny—masseur extraordinaire,
bringer of happy endings—sizes up the shoal, cards in hand.

Not a whiff of Shadow Cabinet: two arthritic backbenchers
and the pro-fracking man off *Newsnight*, drumming

his freebie pen against a mug. What's a merboy to do?
Outside, the weather bludgeons photo ops with cloud,

an Atlantic juggernaut of wind. A bored policewoman
enters in a stab vest, holding a semi-automatic carbine.

Danny slips the cards away, edges inside a tour group
from Graz, reminded suddenly of this year's Pride,

the first float in the parade, how he could think only
of a bomb tucked underneath, its bloom of devastating light,

a microsecond of scorch and then the dark.
Oh I know, it's absurd, says a journalist on her phone

beyond the glass before dodging a stream of Austrians,
the café suddenly quiet. Danny orders a soya latte, waits

by the policewoman who reaches to collect her tea,
so close for two seconds he can hear her breathing.

Michael

Are you visiting this city, or do you live here?

> *The light licks me over, spits me out.*

Can you be more specific?

> *Severe cuts to sunsets except for those who most deserve them.*

And during your stay, what types of accommodation have you used?

> *Doorways. Burger King. Futon in the house of grabby hands. Igloo (invisible).*

What factor has most affected your choices in this regard?

> *How much I'm scaring the customers.*

Is this the only destination on your trip?

> *All the sky in my head. I can float through for days.*

How many nights will you spend here?

> *It's impossible to kill yourself by holding your breath.*

What help have you used to navigate the city?

> *Six little packets of tomato ketchup.*

Please be serious: what help?

> *On the glass of the old phone box, an atlas with islands of poster glue and grease.*

Which of the local attractions have you liked the most?

>The eyes growing in clusters on trees that open gradually, and
>>hold a gaze.

Total cost for your trip?

>*Yes.*

What would you say to other potential visitors?

>*The sea is always sorry. It is talking in its sleep.*

Pterodactyl

'The common term for the winged reptiles properly called pterosaurs'
livescience.com

The fossil behind the glass is lying.
    This twisted backbone makes the creature
bisect herself as though devouring
    her own finger. And the resemblance
to a flung-down puppet misleads. It suggests
    that her jagged roof of wings

was always inadequate shelter, that she never saw
    volcanoes snuffed under her umbrella.
Likewise, the connotations stamped
    last week across the features of the teenager
who laid his hand against the case
    are far from honest. The swelling

beneath his left eye—a traffic light
    that shifts from plum to mustard, pink—
says no more about him than the concealer
    swiped across it. The split lip

that crusted will soon drop its pretence
　　just as the five days he spent ossifying

in his box room in the dark will undress down
　　to one memory of rewatching *Finding Nemo*,
a thin pillar of shine between his drapes.
　　The panic he felt at the prospect
of expeditions beyond his doorstep is sizzling
　　irretrievably in the crater of this trip;

it lifts away like steam. If you believe
　　you caught him gnawing himself,
he was probably taking off excess balm.
　　Under the peak of his cap, what was fragile
before the bruises, what would never fit—
　　and here's a thump or three to demonstrate—

rises to meet the world again, a colour
　　as necessary and true as the orange-red
of magma, the cream of undried bones,
　　the wind-blown blue of cornflowers
beside his neighbour's gate, their small wings
　　pitching and climbing, over and over.

Stones

Rain makes me travel into myself. I lie in bed and notice things: how each fingernail is a screensaver of somewhere I've never been, a white hill beneath a giant sky of pink ghosted with cloud, a country my hands have dreamed.

I have fixed many names to this body across the years— prophet, demon, twit. Once: palace of failures. *The mice behind the skirting sing like birds*, I thought, *but I can't hear them.* The sycamores, too, for all I knew. My body—what a vessel to be stuck in! What a gruesome vase that kept on dribbling through all its holes so I had to rinse it every day until I died.

Later I found it harboured other cargo, stealthy freight concealed beneath my liver's right lobe. A crystalline accumulation—doubts that had condensed into certainties. I woke at 3 a.m. with an angular pain below my sternum, radiating to my back. I phoned a taxi with one hand clutched to my useless, breaking torso. I thought of Carnea,

Roman goddess of organs and door handles, how I'd grown one inside me and it was forcing me open.

Surgeons expanded me with gas, used forceps to coax out my secrets. I came to as someone rattled peppercorns inside a jar. Enough there to build a house!

Wounds made my body tight, my walking speed roughly zero miles per hour. This, however, is the stone of it: there was a door in the middle of the desert. I noticed things— snails sliding up walls, the shape of bricks, how a roof can talk with sky. How every stem and slab and footstep's a sinewed thought of a world that keeps imagining.

I do not need another vessel to better comprehend the dark. I am already part of it, already sending out white hills to join leaves falling, to bump along with tuneful mice singing through the night, with every pebble that begins among a family deep inside this public earth.

Spout

Some months all my thoughts are one colour.
I hit a yellow mood and the world pours out its yolks:
tall stacks of *National Geographic* in Oxfam,
cranes that point uncertain fingers at the sky

while maple leaves swoop into me and cling, their veins
like roads heading everywhere in fallen, saffron cities.
Then, the teapot you saw on eBay, had to have.
It was like unpacking October and standing it on our table,

its yellow logic strict yet plump, offering an outsized handle,
a colour that might foster never-ending cups. We filled it
with boiling water, our new sun, and that first time
the copper rings around its centre made it tick-tick-tick

as if letting us know it could wipe us out if it wanted to
but we'd been spared, that we could live beside it
though should be grateful for everything of its kind
which travelled toward us, all the yellow days.

The Sandman

This body is my deluded hero   It refuses to accept it's dissolving
that my lungs and pancreas   so snug in their cavities   will be unhomed
Sometimes *living* seems like another word   for vanishing
cells crumbling   my skin burlesquing off   carbon flaming away
in every breath   I've been on fire since 1978   I need signs above my exits
Thank you for attending the conference   while the walls of this gathering
of bone persist   with their own slow departures   their molecules
bringing to life my dream   of becoming a flock of goldfinches
Up up up   This structure made of broken stars   keeps being called back
to its origins   No wonder they say outer space   smells human
diesel barbecue gunpowder   Down here   I try hard to be sensible
and worship flux   I devoted one winter morning   to washing clocks
sponging a path for the violence of seconds   erasures worked by quartz
that can't stop itself shaking   I read all the right books   *The murderer's*
flayed skin was turned into leather   and used to bind a series of notes
on his dissection   His punishment   to remain a tangible object
Secretly though the body is my reckless god   I follow its tenets
without thinking   A snowman's face fell off   and I set out instantly
to mend his smile   combing the slush for eyes and teeth I knew
would drop again   Now it's summer   I stride around a garden perfumed
like outer space   I pause to soak up a woodpecker's delirious laugh
that disappears but stays   I watch ants scatter   whilst I stand here
like a pillar of sand   and my body cascades   and does not cascade into air

Please Don't Touch Me, My Head Falls Off

reads the sign around the neck of the enormous Playmobil figure.
I know the feeling. I blame Red Bull and I blame the news.
In tests, 70% of humans can be persuaded to give an electric shock
to a stranger. I'd rather give them shortbread, or perhaps a little wave,

but those too could have blue consequences. I scan the crowd
and wonder who might push the button. This student in brogues,
wielding lilies? The yummy mummy with a fearsome ponytail?
I'm not answering further questions till my solicitor is present

or I have proof they are irrevocably bad, like at that fancy dress party
when I saw a Cyberman smoke a cigarette. Meanwhile, I'm petrified
of the thump in my chest that is four valves closing, that conjures up
a backwards Advent calendar, a door shut with every year.

I tremble, pick at falafel wraps and store each terror
like those bald eagles who save every twig they find
till their overburdened nests plummet to the ground.
I drop my leftover wrap in a bin and consider death by falling

or electrocution. Death by milk float, steered by the nemesis
I didn't know I had. I am vastly misjudged as a foe,
I want to tell him. He doesn't know who he's dealing with,
how much I'm not here, startled as I am by what turns out to be

moss tumbling from gutters, by the voice shrieking and howling
in my pocket that is Kate Bush, by a horde of breakable creatures
not licking or hitting each other, just treading their way
softly along the back of morning, tiny hearts jolting.

Sungazer

It gathered when I was twenty-four, an infection
from a contact lens. The pink halo around one iris,

my dread of light. A searing bulb had the gaze
of a basilisk. Watching TV was like staring into a volcano;

my eyes boiled in their sockets. Like an arachnophobe,
I knew how many gleams there were in a room,

where they hid. I smothered windows with newspaper,
made my bedroom a dungeon. *Let me vanish.*

The infection went, the problem stayed. I visited
a local clinic: chin rests, slow voices, drops

of fluorescein to stain my corneas. Good news,
announced the doctor: he couldn't find any problems.

This didn't sound good to the thing that wore
sunglasses indoors, that on dates blew out

the restaurant's candles. *Bury me in the cellar.*
I stopped leaving my room, became obsessed

with those fish that live at the bottom of the ocean
in total darkness, how natural selection breeds change:

sensitivity to the slightest shift in pressure,
jaws with rows of colossal, impossibly curved teeth.

I dreamed of looking in mirrors at my towering fangs,
my wincing eyes enormous, my skin covered

in small, brilliant scales it hurt to see.
A therapist suggested I gaze at a burning match

for five seconds, build up slowly. I put a time in my diary
each day for watching TV for two minutes.

It felt like counting down to execution. *Finish me.*
It worked. I was not killed by Anne Robinson

or the nine o'clock news. I ordered table lamps
of every kind, coloured bulbs. I left my dungeon.

Now I exist in the realm of light again, I understand
there are times when it is necessary to approach

a blazing house and enter, times when I must open
my eyes wide and let in every quickening flame.

Strange Stories and Outlandish Facts

In Tokyo, you said, *some crows*
build nests from coat hangers.
Are you aware, though, the scaffolding
crowded with danger signs
behind your Heathrow office
is a waterfall of exclamation marks?

You should have sauntered out
ten minutes back. I lurk
beside glass doors till my other self
looks airsick, then wobble
to the coffee bar across the road,
willing your text to land.

Fact, from the 1530s, meaning
thing made, thing done.
Like when you fix small wheels
to my foolishness so it turns
into a vehicle we drive about in.
You fill up my desire to race

to the museum shaped like a teapot,
and not bother with the church
that is a cup. Breathe in this direction,
please, and we can crackle
like those winding lines of cherry trees
in Yoshino's springtime forest—

forks of pink lightning when viewed
from the sky. *Fact*, meaning evil deed.
The Aztecs flaunted necklaces
of popcorn and measured drunkenness
on a scale of rabbits and must
have been delightful on the days

they weren't slicing people open.
I prefer to wear impatience
like a hula hoop in café queues,
slamming into other patrons.
I apologise too many times.
It's a lesson in context; a man can strut

in glass armour but if he goes
to war he'll end up as melody.

Every fact's contingent, fleeting.
On this window, the Boeing 767
overhead appears in each raindrop
as though it's laid planespawn

and is leaving its young behind.
I wouldn't have things otherwise.
I need my blurry edges, a chance
to figure out while speaking
what I'm trying to say, which is simply
that I want your primate warmth

beside my neck, your slim fingers
against the bones and muscles
of my back—its scapulae,
trapezius and all the other parts
with Latin names there is no
earthly need for me to know.

The Orange Trees of Now

I am lounging outside The Honey Locust in my black shirt
as if dressed for the funeral of winter though, actually,
I'm glad it's dead. Really, I'm stuffing my face with quiche
at its wake and hoping for money, to forget it existed.

Spring is falling from the sky and even an empty packet
of Monster Munch trills the news. By the kerb,
there are scattered aquarium stones, green and orange,
like someone from My Little Pony took a dump.
I am sitting here beside my Earl Grey and thinking
how *orange* has its roots in *naranja*, a citrus tree
that sprang from an elephant's corpse.

I too would like to be useful after death, to hand on
kidneys and vim—but that's for another hour.
I am thirty-eight. My newborn grey hairs have prospects.
Come in and talk to Vicki about your barnet!
says the advert next door. Maybe I will.
Maybe I will ask her about arched fringes and Brexit

and other concepts I would not kiss, about the man asleep
a few tables away who may not be breathing
though he doesn't smell yet. In the generous society
I'm part of, dead people are welcome too.

It's so much kinder than it ought to be, this icy pastille
of sun and the teenager with blue pigtails who dips
a coat hanger into a bucket of marbled water and spawns
a lengthy bubble. It drifts along the street like it's just swum
down from the clouds, gathering acolytes as it quivers
then twists stubbornly into the future, heading north.

What Chaos Angels Eat for Breakfast

River likes the squeeze of mornings:
>   everyone jammed

into the kitchen.
>   Dodo and her ladyfriend dismember Twitter

over figs.
>   Crooning, Wayne hoists lazy syrup from the tin,

a cataract descending
>   in slow motion
>   to pancake pools.

CJ, post-ket, tips out a smoothie and misses the glass.

Bonebag!
>   Mauve slush speeds to the floor, a B movie fugitive.

How glorious they are, the fam,
>   with their misadventures—

chaos angels from desiccated towns who crashed mid-flight
and now spice each other's hours.

Later, there will be shadow—jobseeker's segregation,
lobbed iPhones
       and sputtering hearts not even Beyoncé
or butterscotch vodka can fix,
          at least not straight away—
but right now is a mug of lovely noise.
             Let outside
do what it will.
      It is 9 a.m.
         The world is just beginning.

Soulcraft

It's true: there is a light at the centre of my body.
If I could, I would lift aside a curtain of this flesh
and demonstrate, but for now it is my private neon.
It is closest to the air at certain moments,
like when buttercups repair a morning's jagged edge.
Other times, a flock of days descends
and my soul flickers, goes to ground.
Without light, I'm all membrane; each part
becomes a gate. I pour across each margin
and nothing has enough hands to catch me,
my teeth knocking so fast I daren't hold any piece
of myself near in case I start a banquet.
I'm only eased by accident. On the drenched path,
I pick up snails and transport them to safer earth
then feel a stirring. I watch as rain streams
from lopped-back elms, my face teeming with water
and—*hello stranger*—my soul glides to my surface
like it, too, belongs there, like a bright fish rising to feed.

The Weeping Gaga Speaks

He moves her Ladyship into the flat—
a Gaga poster tacked above his bed.
A sunken waif, two inky tears
corrupt a powdered cheek,
her eyes black as an addict's.

Hour after hour, they bore into him
as he swaps trackies, lifts weights,
gulps juice. She eavesdrops while he whispers
the day's sins to the phone, her face tender,
unshockable—weeping still.

When her voice arrives, she wails
incessantly that it's not right,
how she's small and boring, unworthy
of a place on his wall. *It devastates me,*
the way you cradle that glass...

Some nights the sobbing's so intense
she shakes loose from her pins.
A mass of sleek, black hair crashes
onto his body. He wakes at 4 a.m., smothered,
her eyes pressed to his own.

He props Gaga on a chair, explains how,
secretly, he's humdrum too—
how he invents most of this stuff
as he goes along—but she won't have it.
It is terrible to be a god and listen.

Are the Circles Clearer on the Red or the Green?

Dear John. Firstly I would like to say sorry for addressing
you as Japan in my previous email. My various islands

> accept your apology graciously. It's understandable.
> I am an archipelago that's never sure where I lie.

There is always another interview with fifty questions
I can't answer like *Why do you want to work here?*

> *How can I help you today? Do you like the taste*
> *of watermelon?* I'm pure weather. My too-much heart

is a parliament of vapour, fried by its own lightning.
I keep coming to, halfway across the Pacific.

> In department stores, I catch the laser gaze
> of the security guard and believe I am a thief,

unresolved as to whether to half-inch a plain tie
or a striped, or perhaps the cocked trilby of the man

who stares at himself in the badly lit mirror, raising
one hand to the shadow landscape of his face.

A Floating Head

Freed from my shoulders, I drifted
    through the gaping window,
        my thin moustache brooming the air.

I was promising as a shut peony.
    I'd spent so many hours already levitating
        above my body, uncertainly belonging,

it was a relief to turn out to be
    a new species away from the riotous pits,
        those granite slabs of feet, the carping

of a restless cock. I marauded
    through droplets of mist like brother
        full stops loosed from sentences.

I hung in the sky, timeless
    as though I were on a stamp, enjoyed
        regal delusions: a heartless overseer

gauging my state, obstacles
　　to revolution. (*Off with his*. Oh.)
　　　　Heartless, but then ever more gutless.

Oddly exposed without my hands,
　　I perched beside starlings politely
　　　　on lichened roofs. I gravitated

to the immaculate rows of cabbage fields,
　　alighted between fine fellow heads
　　　　to nap, before wandering like a planet

back to where I began. I orbited
　　the little boat of flesh I'd left
　　　　capsized and naked among crumbs

on the kitchen lino when I could carry
　　no more anchors, digest no more
　　　　incursions, no more of my latest

graceless response, the oozy flailing
　　and mutinous pulse of a machine
　　　　so prone to falling, so primed

for defeat and a kiss from the shiny tip
      of the world's meat hook... I stopped
            flying and nestled like a cricket ball

into one palm, felt on my cheek
      the clumsy brush of fingers. I tasted
            dried sweat in their creases and lay there

for a few seconds, knowing it was over,
      that I had no choice but to put myself back—
            return to my sad attachment and try again

to understand the weight of being bodied,
      all the swollen and tender exchanges
            that ground me here, among the living.

Pelican

December nights, I hold anxiety in front of me, electric yellow,
like a giant beak. It smacks into things. The milk I splash
in my tea becomes a jellyfish and that entails being stung,
which takes me to a neat image of death, a Weeping Angel
on the horizon then suddenly at my shoulder, enfolding me
in its wings. I look up at stars that aren't there, that raced off
millennia ago, rushing as far away as they could.

On TV, there is a beluga whale that mimics human voices
and the carrying of objects. I, too, imitate but keep dropping
the objects and screeching in avian fashion, my throat pouch
trembling, my mind always suspecting *Have you got a cigarette*
will lead to *Give me your wallet*.

                                        Then my beak smacks
into something else. I remember the Victorian zoologist
who drew jellyfish on all his Christmas cards like dazzling
chandeliers. Festive tentacles. From my broken fairy light,
a genie of smoke arises, my lover's voice on the phone.
I'm not a bird at all but a man drawn on folded wrapping paper,
cut out and pulled into fifteen of myself by his *hello baby*.

Silkworm

So we stroll down Kings Road, past the stamping beat
of a drag queen at her sewing machine. Lines of stitches on rayon

structure her illusion, the gorgeousness they see before each
        putdown's
needle. The root of *glamour* is *grammar*, you say—a thought

that amuses us as we move beyond the cafés' hubbub
to where fake Regency houses flaunt balustrades and stucco,

concealing the lads on Grindr. (Good luck boys!)
I prize these mazy streets, how they let us collide

with a jogger who happens to be Kat from your office,
directing mice inside her muscles. Here we never go straight

to the point—the lane's always strewn with vomit, blossom,
the latest soaring personae under construction. There's no
        moment

of departure anyway and shoot me if I ever claim I've arrived.
It's getting late as we pass the West Pier, its grand collapse

that whispers *founder* is the root of *fonder*, that the ocean
will swallow this city at length. We, too, have devastating impact,

not just travelling down the path to mine but altering it,
disturbing the air with our daring legs and devious brains.

Montaigne called the mind a silkworm, entangling itself in its
thread.
He came to the disco five centuries too soon. *Clubs make me feel*

ancient, you reply. Well, my house is small but there's glitter
and voltage, and you're always welcome in its white rooms.

Tonight, the Hours Arrive Like Animals

trotting up to give the street a sniff. They curl around the roofs
with clumsy feet, thrilling sycamores, agitating those asleep—
hairdressers, air stewards and pale decades that rest

beneath the ground. I love them all, the same as I love the woman
with slicked-back hair who, in weak light, guides the first
no. 2 bus, who vapes at a shelter where no one waits,

puffs out blueberry fog and types on her smartphone
Sorry about yday angel before returning to the slow rise
of the coast road. It wanders in absurd isolation,

a lost dressing gown cord beside the wind-bitten edge.
Here, in landslides after rain, a room can plunge irreversibly,
floorboards, pillows and coat hangers scattered over the rocks.

The chalk face reveals antique calamities—bison and mammoth.
Each one stirs my overdue love. Rock bolts and soil nails
can't stop the cascade of flint, attention-grabbing tears

beside the waves' discreet rollings. The shivering skyline
is an enormous mammal's pelt you might run a hand along.
Though it doesn't care, I love this fractal coast

and all the torch-lit old men who right now swing
metal detectors above pebbles. I love their stubbornness,
discovered pennies, the oscillating currents of their chatter:

Sharp today ain't it?   Another necklace.
Try eBay.   Shame what happened to Colin.
I love euphoric dogs, spaniels that hoover scents,

black noses aroused by the eyeless corpses of wagtails,
paperbacks crusted in salt and barmen off their heads on crystal,
gripping each other's bodies, convinced they're the only humans left.

My love won't help them but it's there. Just above,
the hotels have gathered to watch the smash of waves
and the wind is another clubber stumbling down St James's Street

past the first commuters. I cherish them all, the kind and heedless,
the spooked and the riot grrrl with the shaved head who, at daybreak,
steps over fugitives from gull-ripped bin bags and hauls up

the pizzeria's rattling shutter, unmoved by the freight train's
retreating voice, too intent to care that the sea through the branches
of beech trees is a hundred minute seas. They hover together

like stained glass, in their own lead-lined way as irrepressible
as the ocean without the frame, incomplete without the distant piece
of the observer, and the falling hours that slide away like animals.

Cartoons for Adults

Last night, scores of red oak leaves descended
        into our garden, a fleet of 2-D spaceships. They parked
haphazardly beneath the black-eyed Susan vine

that once looked dead but now's a fog of orange blooms.
        It's like living in a colouring book, an overall effect
you have a hand in, fella, drawing secret faces on slate chips,

crying *Ahoy there sailor!* to whoever I wake up as,
        even when I've lost my naval hat. There's no dodging it.
In the newspaper, Brighton Pier photographed from above

looks like a scruffy robot fish that survived a cataclysm.
        Time itself is chirpy. We play Frisbee in the park
despite the fact that, when I throw, it veers off

with no chance for you to catch it, rejoining
        the planet's surface fifty metres away as I notice myself
doing lately, wrapped up in the 18-certificate movie

of us that's somehow still closer to Pixar than Fincher,

      more noisette than noir. We keep visiting the same

Japanese restaurant miles from home just to watch

the conveyor belt with its spectrum of covered bowls,

      a procession of small worlds that carries assorted forms

of logic, that circles lazily, season after season.

Accidents

Oh yes the wind blows all kinds of things down
to our basement garden—
    bits of Yorkie wrapper,
coins,
        sometimes whole alphabets and civilizations.
The Second Ant Age begins but you're unvexed.
You thrive beside emergencies,
  by eruptions
of seagulls and this pennywort vine that revels
in throwing itself about
                    as if its beauty were inevitable,
like those lorryloads of bottles
  dumped in the sea
that formed a beach of glass pebbles.
I am an unwieldy object thrown toward you
that you somehow keep managing to catch,
    a string
of accidents you solve, each one folded and stored,
though I feel I could do more

        like not picking
at my joints, not setting myself on fire.
It really is so tasty and educational to live with you,
ousting empires
  or just sipping tea from chipped mugs
and listening to rain,
        to the clouds' magnificent collisions.

Bugsong

It's hard to ignore a musical penis,
this water boatman that drags
his insect prick against the sacred corrugations
of his belly. The males are out in force tonight:
oar-shaped legs and all the niceties of dreadnoughts.

For these are not the tunes of mouths,
not shaped to curl through the cave
of an ear. Each pneumatic chirp's off-key,
strives to shipwreck the listener

with certainties—a spam attack
of aural cock pics, the gaps between
the molecules of pond their glory holes.

They scrape beside each other
in seismic orchestras, masters of disharmony,
each segmented player clutching
his instrument, hell-bent to club down the rest
or scratch his dick out, yank himself to the grave.

In summer, the tattooed sons burst
from eggs and grip their packages
as soon as they can, all set to thump
the masses and that soloist who always wins,
to interrupt the melody of Nobody's racket,
the patient silence that thickens and rises.

Your Kindness Has Snapped Me Like an Old Deckchair

It scrubs all meaning from the seafront's smudged
       white walls, seeping rust, drain covers. No dog turd is safe.

Your kindness: it's lodged behind my eye like a contact lens.
       It contradicts me so I become a local government—

always in the wrong. I have snapped but am repaired.
       Where is the gangrene, the lopped-off feet, my sack

of blood and spit? Now everything is surf-swash-lollipops.
       I demand a full refund. Look, I was fine hanging out

in my lair of driftwood, watching sunsets in broken mirrors,
       admiring leaves on birches in the North Laine—tiny
          plasters

for the sky. Lately, they're all part of your scheme:
       cups, rock pipits, moss—unflagging conspirators that
          strive

to assist each stubborn picnic. I'm not safe even underneath
        a blanket. I don't know what you think you're playing at

but kindly stop. Or, at the very least, keep taking it
        so far I stay helpless; keep dropping soft meteorites

and I'll pretend my head hasn't been repeatedly struck
        as I lie on the beach from dawn till dusk with puzzle
        books

and ruthless company in every weather, my limbs
        encrusted with glowing salt like an old deckchair.

Mumpsimus

'postman's knock ... has nothing to do with dead men at the door'
Rebecca Perry, 'Pow'

Someone left a dictionary on the wall outside my house:
a gift, a threat. The wind rifles through, flumps back,
unsure it has the right first letter. Leaving home, I'm snagged

by words—not meanings but the images they unfold.
Flap dragon, an angry letterbox. *X-ray slap*, make-up
that shows you're broken. I come to streets away

with no memory of walking there. Lost language always seems
to lead to lost time, to endless trekking, fruitless searches.
If I could find the perfect word this would all be over.

It often seems so close I swear if I keep talking
it will tumble out, the something on which it all depends.
I pause merely to cool down, prevent combustion.

The dictionary's mislaid its spine and cover so, when shut,
might be mistaken for a block of ice. Each word's retrievable,
could lead to magic. The decline of the jellygraph

as a copying device and measurement of fear doesn't mean
we shouldn't say *jellygraph* at every given chance.
The dictionary lies open in thunderstorms, its sodden pages

catching syllables. *Coracle*, an underwater prophet.
Rum peeper, the reflection at the bottom of a glass.
I keep thinking of the leap month that appeared in certain years

in Rome, whether it might arrive again if its name
were spoken often enough. *Mercedonius...*
Sun-dried, the dictionary's pages curl, begin to yellow.

Sad beast: no one wants its dreams. I stroke its binding
before I head inside and forget about it for a while,
this wounded animal I can't contain, beyond all help.

A Walk with Our Imaginary Son

for Roddy Lumsden

Rhinoceros vase, bubble turnip, wedding cake venus.
Yes, he is definitely our son, rattling off seashells
between anecdotes from a year well-spent at uni—
his first bar job, first spliff and lots of things
I never did with girls. We've met him in Pavilion Gardens
to show him punks and jugglers, his wild inheritance.
Pavilion, from the Latin *papilio*, moth or butterfly,
and, later, a tent with two flaps, a word fluttering
who knows where. The grass today is full of legs
that might escape their owners, long beings
that reach for each other. The trees, too, are a photograph
of a party—frozen small talk and sneezing and tears
of laughter as we walk through their shadows
and he lists the names: *lime, Dutch elm, plane.*
I study his face, the nose I saddled him with,
the cryptic Lumsden eyes, a moon-sized laugh.
Did you know every shadow has a negative weight?

No I didn't, I say, but I can well believe it, reminded loosely
of how a moth feels on my hand, how there are no words
for the difference it makes to have him here, how we've built
a special tent and now it's flying. But the evening
    approaches.
We don't want him to miss his train. This circuit of the park
will be the last. We slow our pace and watch
the shadows advancing from our feet, certain things
with philosophies, dominions; nothing like moths.

The Skeleton Flower

It exists: a herb that turns to water
in every downpour, each milky bloom
rapidly transparent. Tonight I sit
beside an open window and watch
a street where poplars and blocks
of cellular flats undress themselves
in mizzle, the sudden clarities of bark
and brick exposing phloem tubes
and lusty hands and kitchen discos
while I look down and each bone
and muscle simplifies, my lungs,
heart, guts now limpid verbs,
continuing their selfless work.
It is a privilege to float above such
loyalties amid a forest of descents,
this liquid interval of scatterings
and revelations where a monster lives.
I always wanted to be harmless
but it's plain to me at present

even flowers are not so; most especially
flowers are not so with their giant
thirsts and fantasies and ruthless ways
with light. And I see that if
I am water, I am the dead pigeon
beneath a Volvo, the sweat that gathers
in the creases of a sofa sleeper's brow
and this hoverfly that tugs
itself in angled lines, a cursor
that clicks on each part of my garden
to see if it will open, as the spent
drops bead the railings and the final
cascades plunge from roofs and I stare
at the heavy petals of my hands
that are turning slowly white.